ℬ *Still Life with Buddy* ℭ

by Lesléa Newman

Selected Titles by Lesléa Newman

Poetry Collections
Love Me Like You Mean It*
Sweet Dark Places*

Short Story Collections
Every Woman's Dream
A Letter to Harvey Milk
Secrets

Novels
In Every Laugh a Tear
Good Enough to Eat
Fat Chance

Nonfiction
Writing from the Heart: Inspiration & Exercises for Women
        who Want to Write

Anthologies
My Lover is a Woman: Contemporary Lesbian Love Poems
A Loving Testimony: Remembering Loved Ones Lost to AIDS

* denotes title is available from Pride Publications

❧ *Still Life with Buddy* ☙

A novel told in fifty poems
by Lesléa Newman

Published by Pride Publications
Radnor, Ohio

Still Life with Buddy
copyright 1997 by Lesléa Newman
published by Pride Publications

ISBN 1-886383-27-8

First edition October 1997.
9 8 7 6 5 4 3 2

Author's photograph by Mary Vazquez.
Cover photograph by Cris Newport.
Cover model Walter Morrison.
Cover and interior design by Pride Publications.

Printed in the United States of America.

Pride Publications is a four imprint, international organization involved in publishing books in all genres including electronic publications, producing games, toys, video and audio cassettes as well as representing authors and artists through syndication and as literary agents. The lion and cradled inverted triangle logo are trademarks of Pride Publications. Logo design by Adam Gage and Daniel Gilman.

Pride Publications
Post Office Box 148
Radnor, Ohio 43066-0148.

PridePblsh@aol.com
http://members.aol.com/pridepblsh/pride.html

For My Buddies:

Gerard Rizza
(October 20, 1959 - April 4, 1992)

Stan Leventhal
(May 24, 1951 - January 15, 1995)

Victor Fane D'Lugin
(August 6, 1945 - August 13, 1996)

Contents

Epilogue

ର   *Prologue*   ଓ

Prophecy

When you get in the nineties, my grandmother said
all the people you know are already dead
In 1990 I turn thirty-five
most of my friends more dead than alive

Still Life with Buddy

Attitude Adjustment

I am a negative person
A very negative person
I have always been a negative person
My mother said, "Don't be so negative."
My father said, "Accentuate the positive."
I said, "Expect the worst.
If it happens, you won't be disappointed.
If it doesn't happen, you'll be surprised."
When Buddy got tested
I decided to think positive
I decided to have a positive attitude
I was positive that Buddy was negative
Surprise

○S

A Tale of Two Brunches

1982
Buddy orders brunch fit for a growing boy:
pile of pancakes
heap of homefries
batch of bacon
I order the anorexic special:
lemon tea
Sweet 'n Low on the side
"Aren't you hungry?" Buddy asks
Of course I'm hungry
I haven't eaten in a week
Buddy knows this
It worries him
"You gotta eat if you wanna live,"
Buddy reminds me
as if it was that simple
He makes our waitress bring me
a tower of toast
and pretends not to notice
the burnt, buttered bread
sitting on my plate
untouched, unwanted, ice cold

1992
I order brunch fit for a growing girl:
pile of pancakes
heap of homefries
batch of bacon
Buddy orders the AIDS special:
lemon tea
straw on the side
"Aren't you hungry?" I ask
Of course Buddy's hungry
He hasn't eaten in a week
I know this
It worries me
"You gotta eat if you wanna live,"
I remind him
as if it was that simple
I make our waitress bring him
a tower of toast
and pretend not to notice
the burnt, buttered bread
sitting on his plate
untouched, unwanted, ice cold

ℂ𝔖

The Politics of Buddy

I.
Buddy and I cruise the make-up
at Macy's. I swipe a lipstick
tester across my mouth
Buddy does the same.
We try eyeshadow, mascara
two shades of blush
before a Macy's matron
whose face would crack
a chisel shoos us away.
"Is it a crime for a boy
to wear make-up?" Buddy shouts
"Or is it a crime for a boy
to look so good in it?"

II.
Buddy and Guy saunter down the street
a few beats in front of me.
They do not touch
but their heads bent in boytalk
is enough to slow a car.
Ugly faces leer
"Hey, faggots," "Hey sissy boy,"
"Hey, you goddamn queers."
Buddy yells back, "We're homos.
We're as healthy as the milk you drink,"
then slaps a fat, juicy
kiss on Guy's lips
that no one could possibly argue with.

III.
I take Buddy to Gay Pride
wheeling him carefully through the streets.
A woman bounces up to us
"Where's your red ribbon?" she asks,
fishing out her supply.
Buddy says no thanks
and when she insists he pricks
his thumb with her safety pin.
A thin trickle of blood
oozes down his skin.
"Here's my ribbon.
Is it red enough for you?"
Buddy holds his fist high as I wheel him away.

CஃB

Give What You Can

In NYC on the IRT
Buddy and I sit knee to knee

Man comes in   Eyes the crowd
Clears his throat and speaks real loud

I GOT AIDS!
MY WIFE GOT AIDS!
MY KID GOT AIDS!
WE ALL GOT AIDS!

The train shakes him   He shakes his cup
Urging us to give it up

People drop in coins and bills
Buddy gives two yellow pills

I GOT AIDS!
MY WIFE GOT AIDS!
MY KID GOT AIDS!
WE ALL GOT AIDS!

The subway lurches   Then it stops
Man looks into cup to see what he's got

Doors slide open   Without looking back
He dumps Buddy's meds out onto the track

I GOT AIDS!
MY WIFE GOT AIDS!
MY KID GOT AIDS!
WE ALL GOT AIDS!

Doors slide closed   Train pulls out
Man moves to next car and starts to shout

In NYC on the IRT
Buddy and I sit knee to knee
CB

Plea to Buddy Out for a Drive

Buckle
Up
Don't
Die
Yet
❧

Emergency Room

They say whatever you do
don't look in the mirror
when you're tripping
so of course the first thing
Buddy and I did was look

My face
seemed the same
until it cracked
into a million pieces
and fell on the floor

Buddy's face
simply disappeared
except for his eyes
huge and dark
terrified and terrifying

just as they are right now
⟂

Buddy's Lament

I used to take LSD
Now I take AZT

I used to have lots of lovers
Now I have lots of doctors

I used to stay up all night dancing
Now I stay up all night coughing

I used to drink margaritas on the rocks
Now I drink protein shakes through a straw

I used to sleep in a queen-sized bed
Now I sleep in a hospital bed

I used to have a will to live
Now I have a living will

I used to wonder about previous lives
Now I wonder about future lives

03

Gas Attack

When I open Buddy's door
my nose twitches
and my mother's voice

echoes off the kitchen walls
of my mind: *I smell gas*
nobody light a match

but Buddy's gas is so deadly
I light a match
to kill the smell

and hold the tiny flame
high above my head
like I'm at my first rock concert

overcome with emotion
willing to burn my fingers
down to the bone

if necessary   anything
to stop the show
from being over
⋐

Wheel of Misfortune

Buddy wants to buy a vowel
an eye   so he can see
Vanna White in her tight
blue gown   she turns
the letters on the board
around   the player from Tulsa
can't decide what to do
he's clearly a loser
he hasn't a clue
until the phrase of the day
rolls off Pat Sajak's tongue
into Buddy's waiting ear:
youth is wasted on the young

The Bright Side

no hair
no bad hair days
⚘

Buddy's Pantoum

I sit in the hospital with Buddy
He is thin as the IV pole by his bed
Buddy gasps for breath, holding on for dear life
As his roommate's TV bursts into laughter

He is thin as the IV pole by his bed
His skin is so hot it burns my hand
As his roommate's TV bursts into laughter
Buddy's doctor snaps on two rubber gloves

His skin is so hot it burns my hand
His empty eyes are full of fear
Buddy's doctor snaps on two rubber gloves
loudly, like a teenager cracking her gum

His empty eyes are full of fear
He hesitates, then clears his throat
loudly, like a teenager cracking her gum
He says, "Buddy, when your heart stops...."

He hesitates, then clears his throat
Time stands still in the airless room
He says, "Buddy, when your heart stops
should we let you go or bring you back?"

Time stands still in the airless room
Buddy's lips move but he doesn't speak
"Should we let you go or bring you back?"
The only sound in the world: a commercial for Diet Coke

Buddy's lips move but he doesn't speak
"If you don't decide, we're legally obligated to save you."
The only sound in the world: a commercial for Diet Coke
The doctor peels off his gloves, chucks them into the trash

"If you don't decide, we're legally obligated to save you."
Buddy groans, rolls his head on the pillow, side to side
The doctor peels off his gloves, chucks them into the trash
gives a little wave, leaves me and Buddy alone

Buddy groans, rolls his head on the pillow, side to side
His roommate who always hears everything
gives a little wave, leaves me and Buddy alone
I take his hand, ask him what he wants

His roommate who always hears everything
despite his attempts to appear asleep
I take his hand, ask him what he wants
His voice slow and thick, "I don't know how to decide."

Despite his attempts to appear asleep
I know Buddy is trying hard not to cry
His voice slow and thick, "I don't know how to decide.
I can't think about it now. Tell me a story."

I know Buddy is trying hard not to cry
I rack my brain for something to say
"I can't think about it now. Tell me a story."
"Once upon a time, there was a boy named Buddy."

I rack my brain for something to say
I sit in the hospital with Buddy
"Once upon a time, there was a boy named Buddy."
Buddy gasps for breath, holding on for dear life

✂

Thirteen Ways of Looking at Buddy

I.
Among one hundred AIDS patients
the only moving thing
is the stream of tears
leaking out of Buddy's left eye

II.
I was of three minds
like Buddy's cheek
upon which there are three KS lesions

III.
Buddy tried to move his legs
It was a sorry part of the pantomime

IV.
A man and a man
are one
A man and a man
and a virus
are one

V.
I don't know which to prefer
the noise of pain
or the noise of silence
Buddy's moans
telling me he's still alive
or just after

VI.
Tubes run in and out of Buddy
Barbaric needles pierce his skin
Buddy stares at his monstrous shadow
His mood is indecipherable

VII.
O rich doctors and government officials
as you feast on steak and wine
how can you forget the thin face of Buddy
wrapped around a straw
too weak to sip his water?

VIII.
I know the thrill of my lover's touch
and the delight of magnolias in bloom
But I know, too
that Buddy is involved
in everything I know

IX.
When Buddy flies off to heaven
he will mark the edge
of one of many circles

X.
At the sight of Buddy
lying in a hospital bed
even the most jaded doctor of all
would cry out sharply

XI.
I rode the train to New York
Once unutterable joy overtook me
in that I mistook
the smiling healthy man to my right
for Buddy

XII.
My heart is beating
Buddy must be breathing

XIII.
It was the last day of his life
every day for a week
He was dying
and he was going to die
Buddy lay without moving
under a white cotton sheet

ෆ

Thud

If Buddy falls
in the hospital
and there's no one
there to hear,
has a sound
really been made?

⌀

Buddy's Koan

What is the sound
of one lung
breathing?

CB

Once Upon a Time

Buddy wore a watch
with no hour hand
no minute hand
just a second
hand that swept
round and round
his wrist endlessly.
When I said to Buddy,
"What time is it?"
he always answered, "Now."
Once a beautiful stranger
stopped him on the street
and asked, "Do you
have the time?"
Buddy stretched his arms wide
smiled that smile
"I have all the time
in the world."

I remember the day
Buddy's arm shrank
for all time
and I watched
eternity slip from
his wrist forever
CB

Math Anxiety

If I get out of the 8:59 at 12:03
at 34th and 8th in NYC

If I spend 4 minutes flagging down a cab
that speeds 90 miles an hour down 7th Ave

If I dash 12 flights up to the ICU
bribe 3 or 4 doctors and a nurse or 2

What are the chances that when I arrive
Buddy will still be awake and alive?

ೞ

Famous Last Words

In haiku class
Buddy and I learned
about a zen master

who gathered all his students
to hear his final words.
The students drew close

eager to partake
in the wisdom of the dying.
The master asked

for a cup of tea.
It was brought.
He took a sip.

"The tea is delicious,"
the zen master said
then he died.

Buddy loved that story.
"The tea is delicious,"
he said over and over,

"Remind me
when the time comes
the tea is delicious."

The time came.
Buddy lay in a coma.
All his friends drew near

eager to partake
in the wisdom of the dying.
Buddy didn't move

or speak for days.
Out of nowhere
I remembered, whispered

"The tea is delicious,"
into his sleeping ear.
Buddy's eyes flew open.

He looked at me, said
"This sucks,"
and closed his mouth forever.

03

Rainy Day

Buddy can't sip
so I grip
ice chips
in my fingertips
and slip
them thru the slit
between his lips

Like a girl banking dimes
in hopes of better times

CB

Sestina for Buddy

Oh for the days when AIDS
was a candy cube I ate to lose weight
my only goal in life to be skinny
as Buddy is right now, all eyes
and bones in his hollow face
still lovely in the early morning.

Buddy sleeps all morning
now. Even the hospital aids
pause to stare at his chiseled face.
I sit at his bedside and wait
for him to open his left eye,
the right one lost forever in a fold of skin

swollen and purple like the skin
of a grape. In fact, this very morning
boasts three new lesions I
kiss one by one by one. I'm not afraid of AIDS
only of this never-ending wait
which is sure to end too soon. Will I be able to face

Buddy's death when it comes? His face
is a battleground: mottled skin,
sunken cheeks from lack of weight.
Will this morning be the morning
Buddy loses and AIDS
wins? It's a question I

don't want answered so I focus my eyes
once again on his dear old face,
so familiar yet so strange since AIDS
has rearranged everything under the skin.
Who can bear this sight first thing in the morning?
I swallow hard and wait

for my courage not to fail me, wait
for Buddy to open his one good eye,
wait for the waiting to be over and the mourning
to begin. I memorize his face:
the unbearable translucence of his skin
wracked by this monster we call AIDS.

If I could aid him in ending this wait
to leave his skin behind and fly, I
would face him to the light and let him go this morning

CS

The Zen of Buddy

Sitting on a meditation bench
motionless for hours
eyes closed   hands folded
spine straight as a chopstick
breathing shallow
both feet numb
dying to reach Nirvana

Lying on a hospital bed
motionless for hours
eyes closed   hands folded
spine straight as a needle
breathing shallow
both feet numb
dying to reach Nirvana
⊗

(Pass Me a Rearrange): Lines from Buddy's Poems

I spent all morning alone
in the suburbs of your sheets
My nose is as dry as robbery
feet are stars tied
glasses sweeten my face

You had better buckle
up for what I am almost
going to hurl at you,
most ordinary boy

If I take care of myself forever,
what will you give to me?
What are your pockets full of today?

All we have
is everything
I look to the sky
A light gets into my eyes
The pillow sees it
I'm glad I'm alive

Come near to me
The people never stop moving walk in from
outside up from downstairs
Who is this in my arms?
We might have made an extraordinary team
I'll call you whoever you are
Keep me up on your life

People say ok honey you can go
in a moment you can give it
all up

I had great fun
with great friends old and new
I didn't mean to stay
then say goodbye now take care now
Help yourself to your own life

In case you are not wondering
this begins love's continuous final night

❧

Vital Signs

Rest Area
Quiet Zone
No Standing
Blind Drive
Departures Only
Rough Road Ahead
Slow
Downhill
One Way
Ticketed Passengers Only
No Baggage Beyond This Point
Road Narrows
Stay In Lane
Last Exit
Tunnel
Enter
No U-Turn
Fog
Wooded Area
Light Ahead
Densely Populated
Children At Play
Proceed
Shoulder Disappears
Yield
Stop
Dead End

CB

In Your Dreams

you stroll through the Village,
men turning to stare as you pass.
You are not thinner than Kate Moss

only taller and better dressed.
You are wearing an evening gown
not a hospital gown and a corsage

not a catheter is pinned to your chest.
Your legs still hold you up as a sea
of men parts to let you enter the bar.

The sign above your head says,
"No one is ugly after 2 a.m."
not, "Patient is blind in both eyes."

The stage is dark until you step up
and then a light embraces you
like a halo. You lift the mike

and get caught in the cord
like the IV tubes that are forever
in your way. You start to sing

and your voice soothes
you like the sweet, sad lullaby
your mother never sang. Before

the song ends, a nurse comes to change
your feeding tube, but you refuse
to face this nightmare

of a life and choose instead
to become the angel you always were.
Now in my dreams

you stroll through the Village,
men turning to stare as you pass.
You are not thinner than Kate Moss

only taller and better dressed.
You are wearing an evening gown
not a hospital gown and a corsage

not a catheter is pinned to your chest....

CR

Dream

"Make me one with everything,"
said Buddy to the hot dog man
"You are one with everything,"
said the hot dog man to Buddy
I woke at once to tell Buddy the news
but he was already Enlightened

CZ

Nutmeg

When you were at work   Guy and I grew
bored   but the only drug in the house
to drop was nutmeg
which we did   dumped the whole container
into a milkshake from McDonalds and drank up
nothing happened   no visions no buzz
a total bust   until we went to pick you up
I noticed it first   waiting
at a stop light   a lady
in fake leopard coat walking her Chihuahua
had your face   a kid
on a Schwinn pumping
up the hill   your face on his face   Guy
noticed it too   turned to tell me
he looked just like you   I twisted
the rear view mirror and stared   you stared back
and winked   At the train station   every passenger
getting off the 6:33   a dead ringer
Will the real Buddy please stand up?
Finally you emerged   somehow we knew
and leapt from the car shrieking   smothering you
with hugs and kisses   bowing down
to the homecoming queen   you were pleased
then embarrassed   then suspicious
"What are you guys on, anyway?"
"Nutmeg!" we roared   giggling like girl scouts
Ten years later I take no drugs   still see your face
everywhere   that kid on a skateboard   the boy who
pumps my gas   the UPS man with his fancy clipboard
anyone tall dark   and under thirty
Will the real Buddy please stand up?

I'm still waiting for you   to emerge
from anywhere   oh the hugs the kisses
I would give you   your smile making me higher
than the balloons we released
the day you died   standing on the beach
the ocean a foamy milkshake   Guy's eyes dark wet clouds
the sand under our feet   grainy as nutmeg
Will the real   Buddy please stand up

C8

Flies

Buddy and I discovered hundreds
of Woody Allen size flies
clumped together like quivering blackheads
on the white walls of his bedroom.
"The hell with karma," Buddy yelled
running out to buy two cans of Super Raid
which we sprayed on the walls,
windows, ceiling and carpet.
"Raid kills bugs dead," I said
quoting the commercial
and holding out a paper bag
for Buddy to fill
with half-dead sentient beings
their legs sticky and still kicking
in the dying afternoon.
"What kind of Buddhist am I?"
Buddy moaned, then pointed a finger.
"You started it," he said.
"If I die young, it'll be all your fault."
"Just save me a place in heaven," I replied
and then the matter was dropped
until today
when I take full responsibility
for not saving your life.

∞

Buddy Never

Accepted the fact he was going to die
Blamed himself for being sick
Considered suicide for more than a minute
Dreamed he'd die at thirty-two
Entered a room without turning heads
Forgave himself for being sick
Gave up hope they'd find a cure
Hid his lesions with bandaids or make-up
Injected his meds without making a face
Joked around about losing his hair
Knew how much I really loved him
Lied to anyone about how he got sick
Made up his mind about reincarnation
Named his last T cell Bert or Ernie
Obeyed his doctors when he knew he knew better
Pretended he wasn't extremely afraid
Quit trying to write even when he went blind
Regretted the way he had lived out his life
Shook hands with the priest who wanted to save him
Told anyone he was ready to die
Understood why they hate us so much
Vowed to be good in exchange for more time
Wondered why him and not somebody else
X-ed out the names of his friends who had died
Yelled out loud when the pain got too great
Zoomed out of this world without changing my life

CB

Copy Shop a Go-Go

I give Buddy's photo
to the kid with
Michelangelo's David
tattooed on his arm.
The little prick
near his wrist
twists
and I see the kid
knew Buddy
in a way
I never did
nor wanted to.
"One hundred copies,
and these, too," I say
handing him the poems
Buddy wanted me to read
at his funeral.
The kid turns up the radio
then puts Buddy's face
down on the copier
closes the lid
tight as a coffin
and presses a button.
Things whir and click
like a hospital room,
then something jams
and hundreds of copies
of Buddy's face
shoot straight up,
flapping and fluttering
all about the room.

Everybody stares
as if on cue
the Weather Girls shriek
their disco hit
"It's Raining Men"
as the kid and I leap
up on the counter
and start to weep
reaching up
one last time
to gather Buddy
into our arms.

ℭ℥

The Last Thing I Need

A cab blaring Big Band music
swerves to the curb to pick me up.
"Remember the good old days?"
the cabbie asks. He uses his mirror
to check me out. "Of course
that was way before your time,"
he says. "The good old days:
When gay meant happy and aids
were people in hospitals
who helped the doctors out."
He tries to catch my eye
but I throw him a scowl.
"Why the long face?
A pretty girl like you's got nothing
to be sad about. C'mon
let's have a smile."
My corner comes not a moment too soon.
I fling the door open
before the cab stops. "I'm not happy,
I'm gay," I hiss. "And here's a tip:
next time you don't want to get stiffed
try keeping your big mouth shut."
I dash out of the cab
without looking back
and run like hell to Buddy's funeral.

CB

In the Ladies' Room at Buddy's Funeral

All of Buddy's gal pals
hover about the mirror
fixing feathered lipstick
smoothing smudged mascara

except one woman who smokes
in the corner, avoiding
the mirror like the plague
I try not to stare at

Buddy's mile high cheekbones
Buddy's bedroom eyes
Buddy's double dimples
I imagine she has Buddy's smile

though I can't imagine Buddy's sister
has anything left to smile about.
When she stubs out her Marlboro
I go over to say something

but she stares at me wordlessly
like a deer caught in the glare of headlights
or a thief caught in the blare of sirens
then she bolts from the bathroom

as if she's seen a ghost
which she has:
her own face, beautiful as Buddy's
reflected in both my watery eyes

CB

Still Life with Buddy

mahogany table top
hand-made doily
fluted crystal vase
sprig of forget-me-nots
photo of Buddy dressed to kill
leaning against his ashes

ᘓ

Buddy's Jacket

Buddy's jacket
Buddy's leather jacket
Buddy's black leather jacket
Buddy's black leather jacket with the sixteen zippers
Buddy's black leather jacket with the sixteen zippers:
all of them unzipped

When Buddy wore his jacket
men groaned
women moaned
even dogs followed him home

Buddy would give me
the shirt off his back
but he wouldn't let me touch
The Jacket

it's hanging in my closet now

Like the remains of a snake
who outgrew its skin
and silently slipped away
ॐ

Haiku

Buddy's scarab ring
symbol of eternal life
on my finger now

CƷ

Fun with Buddy's Meds

Pour them
into a jar and shake it
to a Tito Puente tape
Buddy always liked a Latin beat

String them
into necklace & earring sets
and wear them to a drag ball
Buddy did love to accessorize

Feed them
to the rats in the hall
and watch them puke all night
Remember Buddy's sick sense of humor?

Line them
up on a table   take
a hammer   smash them
one by one by one
ॐ

How to Get Through a Day Without Buddy

Wake up
Enjoy the 2.7 seconds before you remember
Remember
Pull the covers over your head
Try to sleep
Pretend to sleep
Wish you could sleep forever
Turn over
Put your pillow over your head
Yell, "Shut up!" to the birds outside your window
Doze
Wake
Stare at the ceiling
Think   *Buddy would want me to get out of bed*
              Buddy would want me to get to my desk
              Buddy would want me to go on writing
              Buddy would want me to go on with life

Think *Bullshit*

Think   *Buddy would want me to never get up*
              Buddy would want me to drown in despair
              Buddy would want me to give up my writing
              Buddy would want me to give up on life

Think *The truth shall set you free*

Smile
Get up
Make coffee
Get dressed
Sit at your desk
Stare at a picture of Buddy
Cry
Miss him
Write a poem about missing him
Decide the poem is awful
Decide the poem is wonderful
Wonder what Buddy would think
Reach for the phone
Enjoy the 2.7 seconds before you remember
Remember
Go back to bed
Pull the covers over your head
Try to sleep
Pretend to sleep
Wish you could sleep forever

CB

Be Careful What You Ask For

Every Sunday morning
Buddy emerged
from the boudoir
jerked his neck
twisted his spine
snapped his elbows
flicked his wrists
pulled his fingers
flexed his toes
each bone cracking loud
enough to wake the dead.
I'd rattle the *Times*
over the racket, shout
"Can't a person have
a little peace and quiet?"
Now each Sunday morning
silent as a cemetery

∝

Dear Sir or Madam

This is just to say
I have eaten
at your restaurant
many, many times
you may remember

a small woman
and a tall man
sitting in the corner
stuffing themselves silly
with chocolate ambrosia

Forgive me
I won't be back
Buddy's dead
and your food
tastes like mud

CB

The Return of Buddy

Buddy's Back!
I was running out
to get cream for my coffee
when I passed a newsstand and stopped
to see what the *Times* and the *Post*
were arguing about this morning
but for once everyone agreed
that the news of the day was Buddy
the mutt from Massapequa
who disappeared a week ago
only to be found this very day
in Denver, Colorado
and flown back to JFK
where his family greeted him
with doggie biscuits
an invitation from David Letterman
and a St. Patrick's Day hat
There are no newspapers in heaven
There are probably talk shows in hell
Buddy, believe me, if you chose to return
I would never meet you at the airport
with something as tacky as a green paper hat
Oh Buddy   we love you   come back
○8

Oscar Night

If I had a dollar
for every red ribbon
pinned to every jacket

and every gown
worn by every movie star
whose billion dollar smile

lit up my living room tonight
I'd be very rich
and Buddy would still be dead
CB

October 20, 1992

Happy birthday, Buddy.
Did they throw a big party for you
in heaven?
Were there lavender balloons everywhere
and white roses in tall crystal vases
and a big chocolate cake
with thirty-three candles glowing
in your eyes?
Was there a chorus of pretty boys
singing happy birthday to you,
their arms outstretched
wine glasses raised high,
your amber reflection in every one?
Was there laughing and dancing
and drinking and cruising?
Did you pick one special boy
to celebrate with
or were there many?
Two years ago
you told me you were dying
to have sex.
"At least I won't need rubbers
in the after life," you said,
no bitterness left in your tired voice.
Oh Buddy, there are no condoms in heaven.
There are no hospital beds, wheelchairs,
or catheters in heaven.
There is no AZT, DDI, KS or PCP in heaven.
Only all those pretty pretty boys like you
who went through hell to get there.

❦

Letter from Buddy, Postmarked Heaven

Darling,
Dying was hell
but death is heaven
There's lots of pretty boys here
even prettier than me
if you can believe it
and we have sex all the time
every hour on the hour if we feel like it
because we're all dead already
so it doesn't even matter
There's a library that's open all the time
with every book you ever wanted to read.
All the great poets are always milling about:
Frank O'Hara, Ezra Pound
Allen Ginsberg, too
Did I tell you the food is fabulous?
I can eat again
anything I want
my heavenly body is good as new
In fact, I had a little nosh
with your grandmother the other day
and she said to tell you
it's enough already
you should get married
have a couple kids
stop being so stubborn, *eppes*
you ain't getting any younger
I told her to get over herself

and she said, all right
matzo balls, gefilte fish
what's the difference
as long as you're happy
Are you happy, sweetheart?
How's my Guy?
Are you taking good care of him
like you took good care of me?
Listen, I gotta go
My dad's taking me fishing
You know I haven't seen him
in twenty years
we've got a lot of catching up to do
So, don't cry for me, Staten Island.
Keep in touch
don't forget me
Remember I want to know
how it all turns out
and when they finally find
the goddamn cure
send a double dose C.O.D./A.S.A.P.
I can't stay up here forever, you know
Sure they call this place heaven
but it simply isn't true
even heaven isn't heaven
without my Guy and you

⚬

Goodbye Old Cat
(for Couscous)

O sweet girl, your time is up
No more vets, no more pain, no more fear
Heaven will be sitting in Buddy's lap
His voice a warm purr in your ear

CB

366 & Counting

someone told me
you only cry
every day
for the first
year

she was wrong
⋐

Mid-life Crisis

Buddy, I'm turning 40 this year
and you know what that means
Soon I'll be too old to win
the Yale Younger Poets Award
Remember you told me I could win
first because I was older than you?
You were convinced it was only
a question of time. Remember
when we got stoned and stayed up all night
trying out titles for your first book of poems?

Buddy and the Beast
The Joy of Buddy
I Was a Teenage Buddy
Portrait of the Artist as a Young Buddy
The Good, The Bad, and The Buddy

Buddy, I'm turning 40 this year
You're still 32
I used to be 5 years older than you
Now I'm 8 years older and counting
I might as well face it
I'm never going to win
the Yale Younger Poets Award
and you're always going to be the prize
the Yale Younger Poets Award
never had a chance to win

CB

Reminder

In case anyone's forgotten
what a brat you could be
let me tell The Quiche Story:

we had gone out for a light supper
Both you and Guy ordered quiche
His piece looked bigger than yours

and always the size queen, you asked
to switch. Guy said no, you threw a fit
and stormed out into the night

We didn't follow. Just finished our supper
(yours, too) and waited. Then went home
and realized you had the only key.

So we sat on the stoop and talked
and laughed and looked at the stars
and talked some more and tried to stay warm

At first we were too mad to be worried
then too worried to be mad
Finally you came home drunk at half past two

said, "Excuse me," and opened the door
as if you were doing us a favor
Guy didn't want to know where you'd been

I didn't have the heart to ask
Buddy, you may be an angel now
But you were never, ever a saint

CB

When You Least Expect It

You're walking down the street
just minding your own business
feeling pretty damn good
for once in your life
You got money in your pocket
food in your belly
and a date with your best girl
later that night
As if all that wasn't enough
you just got a poem published
in a magazine so respectable
you can even show it to your mother
If your life was an MGM musical
you'd probably start singing
"Everything's Coming Up Roses" right now
or "Don't Rain On My Parade"
You turn a corner, come upon a schoolyard
and actually start humming
"Thank Heaven For Little Girls"
for they're everywhere: playing hopscotch
jump rope, swinging on the swings
Suddenly the music changes
and a Miss Gulch-like teacher blows her whistle
All the little girls scurry around
like Keystone Cops
until they're lined up in twos
about to enter Noah's Ark
But wait — one girl's all alone

over by the slide about to sing
"Over the Rainbow"
Miss Gulch blows the whistle on her
and demands she line up RIGHT NOW!
"I can't," says the little girl
"Why not?" Miss Gulch
and inquiring minds want to know
"I can't find my buddy," the little girl wails
and suddenly the floodgates open
and you're bawling your head off, too
no longer the daughter, the poet, the lover
but simply the girl who's just lost her Buddy

∽

What I Did on My Summer Vacation

I got on an airplane in New York
I got off the airplane in San Francisco
I took a taxi to the Castro
I walked down Market Street
I found the NAMES project headquarters
I went inside
I looked around
I saw sewing machines
I saw a volunteer
I asked her how to make a panel
She gave me a pamphlet
She said, "You might want to see if your friend
already has a panel."
She gave me a book
I looked up Buddy's name
It was there
It had a number next to it: 2376
I showed the number to the volunteer
She typed it into a computer
She stared at the screen
She said Buddy's panel was not out on exhibition
She said I could see Buddy's panel
if I came back on Tuesday
I came back on Tuesday
A different volunteer was there
I told her I came to see Buddy's panel
She pointed to a gym bag on the floor
She said Buddy's panel was in there

She said I had to help her unfold it
I helped her unfold it
We hung it on a pole
We hoisted it up on the wall
I stepped back to look at it
It was purple
It had Buddy's name on it
It had Buddy's birthday on it
It had the day Buddy died on it
It had one of Buddy's poems:

> *The story is the way we learned it*
> *staged somewhere as memory's*
> *sympathy what we got after this*
> *time's production was a lake*
> *to blow off on when I tell you*
> *I see you before my lids fall*
> *to silence you are somewhere*
> *else believing in your body*
> *as center or the frame*
> *some manner of memoriam*
> *skillful though not clever*
> *a spirit hangs elfin from*
> *your nose trying to pull you*
> *to the beauties you are about*
> *to leave behind unnoticed*
> *but never unkindly*

I read Buddy's poem over and over
As soon as I got to the end, I went back
to the beginning again

I read Buddy's poem outloud
I read it to myself
I took a picture of it
I wrote it down
The volunteer was nice
She brought me tissues
She brought me water
She said I could stay as long as I wanted
I asked her who made Buddy's panel
She said she didn't know
I asked if she could find out
She picked up the phone
She spoke to someone
She hung up the phone
She said she couldn't tell me
She said it was against the rules
I cried
I asked to see the boss
I tried to slip her a twenty
I swore I wouldn't tell a soul
She said she was sorry
I said I was sorry, too
I put the twenty in the donation box
I went outside
It was sunny
I walked around the Castro
I looked at all the men
Any one of them could have been Buddy
None of them were
I went home

☙

No Place Like Home

At a family reunion
my mother serves alphabet soup
The letters H I V swim before my eyes
I blink: my imagination
or a cruel cosmic joke?
Speaking of cruel jokes
my cousin has one:
One stockbroker says to the other
"I got IBM at 26 and a half."
The other stockbroker says,
"That's nothing. I got HIV at 24 and a half."
Ha Ha Ha
Buddy did not die
laughing

Cʒ

April 4, 1995

I dream Buddy and I make love
in my childhood bedroom for a long, long time.
Afterwards my father comes in and tells us
to hurry or we'll be late for school.
My mother brings me some shoes,
black sandals with very high heels
lots of straps and no back. Slides
my lover would call them. My lover!
She won't like this one bit.
"Are you going to break up with Guy now?"
I ask Buddy. "Does this mean we're straight
after all?" He ignores me and flips
through a magazine, *Glamour* or *Vogue*
each page turning with a loud, sharp crack.
I wake up mad, then glad
because even an indifferent Buddy
is better than no Buddy at all.
I plunge back to sleep
but it's no use:
the dream is gone
I'm wide awake
it's 5:23
the same time Buddy died
three years ago today
ॐ

Ode To a Server: Lunch on Sixth Ave

Guy and I can hardly breathe
let alone order, with you
suddenly at our table
pen and pad posed,
beautifully balanced between
male and female
black and white
adult and child.
You wait puzzled, then dazzle
us further with your smile
which so unnerves Guy
he spills his water
into my lap. You rush off
and return with napkins
that look like flowers
in your strong, delicate hands.
Finally we order and you leave
us to our stunned selves.
Neither of us will say it:
you look just like Buddy
a decade ago when he was
my roommate and Guy's lover
and none of us could imagine
ourselves middle-aged
or dead. Suddenly it is hard
to eat but we order more food
another drink, dessert, anything
to bring you back
to our table one more time.

You bring the check
which we argue over
then tactfully walk away
so we can leave you an obscene
tip neither of us can afford
along with both our business cards.
Guy wonders who you'll call
first. I imagine you adding
our cards to a mile-high stack
teetering in your apartment

or pasting them in place
among the hordes you've fashioned
into adoring wallpaper. But who cares?
Knowing beauty such as yours
still exists in the world
is enough to make Guy and I mad
with joy as we rush out
into the razzle-dazzle street
forgetting just for a moment
how mad we are with grief.

୯ଓ

ജ   *Epilogue*   ഌ

Epilogue

Postscript

By the year 2000, Buddy said,
they'll find a cure, but I'll be dead.
New drugs appear in '96
too late for Buddy, who's no longer sick.

Notes

1. "*(Pass Me a Rearrange): Lines from Buddy's Poems*" is a cut up which consists of lines from the poetry of Gerard Rizza, published in *Regard for Junction* ©1992 Gerard Rizza (Spectacular Diseases, 1992). Used by permission of the literary estate of Gerard Rizza.

2. "Thirteen Ways of Looking at Buddy" was inspired by the poem, "Thirteen Ways of Looking at a Blackbird" by Wallace Stevens.

3. "Dear Sir or Madam" was inspired by the poem, "This Is Just To Say" by William Carlos Williams.

4. "The Return of Buddy" was inspired by the poem, "Lana Turner has collapsed!" by Frank O'Hara.

5. The italicized lines in "What I Did on My Summer Vacation" were written by Gerard Rizza and are used with the permission of the literary estate of Gerard Rizza.

Acknowledgments

Grateful acknowledgment is made to the National Endowment for the Arts for their generous support; to Jennifer DiMarco, Carol DiMarco, Cris Newport, and Joni Wilde of Pride Publications, who worked so hard to bring this book into print; to Walter Morrison for gracing the cover; and to the editors who first published earlier versions of some of these poems in magazines, journals and anthologies, including:

"Buddy's Koan" appeared in *Bay Windows*, June 1, 1995.

"Buddy Never," and "Buddy's Lament" appeared in *This Wood Sang Out*, (published by The Literacy Project, 1996).

"Buddy's Pantoum" appeared in *The Harvard Gay and Lesbian Review*, Spring 1995, Volume II Number 2.

"Buddy's Pantoum," and "Dear Sir or Madam" appeared in *Blue Violin*, Issue # 2, 1996.

"Famous Last Words," "The Last Thing I Need," "Midlife Crisis" and "Be Careful What You Ask For" appeared in *Chiron Review*, Issue #50, Spring 1997.

"Flies" appeared in *Telephone*, Number 18.

"Flies" appeared in *Every Woman's Dream* by Lesléa Newman (New Victoria Publishers, 1994).

"Fun with Buddy's Meds" and "No Place Like Home" appeared in *Diseased Pariah News*, Issue #10, 1995.

"In the Ladies Room at Buddy's Funeral" appeared in *Earth's Daughters*, Issue #45.

"In Your Dreams," "October 20, 1995," and "Nutmeg" appeared in *Art & Understanding: The International Magazine of Literature and Art about AIDS*, Issue 15 Volume 4 Number 2, April 1995.

"October 20, 1995," and "Ode to a Server: Lunch on Sixth Ave" appeared in *A Loving Testimony: Remembering Loved Ones Lost to AIDS,* edited by Lesléa Newman (Crossing Press, 1995).

"Once Upon a Time" appeared in *Evergreen Chronicles*, Spring 1996.

"(Pass Me a Rearrange): Lines from Buddy's Poems" appeared in *Napalm Health Spa*, Report 1996.

"Reminder" and "A Tale of Two Brunches" appeared in *Fireweed*, Issue #56 Winter, 1996.

"Sestina for Buddy" appeared in *Sojourner*, Volume 22, Number 9, May 1997.

"Still Life with Buddy" and "The Return of Buddy" appeared in *Columbia: A Journal of Literature and Art*, Spring 1996.

"Thirteen Ways of Looking at Buddy" appeared in *Journal of Gay/Lesbian/Bisexual Identity*, Volume 1 Number 1, January 1996.

"Thud" and "Haiku" appeared in *Bay Windows*, May 25, 1995.

About the Author

Lesléa Newman is a writer and editor with over twenty books to her credit including the poetry collections, *Love Me Like You Mean It* and *Sweet Dark Places* (soon to be combined in a special edition); the short story collection, *A Letter to Harvey Milk;* and the novel, *In Every Laugh a Tear.* She is the author of a children's book about AIDS entitled *Too Far Away to Touch,* and the editor of an anthology entitled *A Loving Testimony: Remembering Loved Ones Lost to AIDS.* Ms. Newman received a Certificate in Poetics from Naropa Institute's Jack Kerouac School of Disembodied Poetics, where she studied with Allen Ginsberg and Anne Waldman. Her literary awards include Poetry Fellowships from the National Endowment for the Arts and the Massachusetts Artists Foundation. Four of Ms. Newman's books have been Lambda Literary Award Finalists. A native New Yorker, she now makes her home in western Massachusetts.

Visit the author's web page at:
http://members.aol.com/lezel/leslea.html

Pride Publications
bringing light to the shadows
voice to the silence

Our History
Pride Publications was founded in 1989 by a circle of authors and artists. A publishing house dedicated to shedding light on misconceptions, challenging stereotypes and speaking for those not spoken for. A press created for the authors, artists and readers, not for profit. With several imprints and divisions, Pride publishes books in all genres by all kinds of authors, regardless of gender, orientation, race or age. We are always looking for new projects that are revolutionary in content. At Pride we believe that risk and diversity are part of life. We believe in opening eyes.

Our Facts
Pride Publications works with artists, authors looking for publishers, authors self-publishing who want help, and authors in need of agents. Authors published with Pride receive 10-15% of gross monies received and retain the rights to their book. Authors will also have say in all edits, artwork and promo done for their book.

Authors co-publishing with Pride's help pay only half of the paper costs. Pride pays for all other costs and offers all standard services including accounting, advertising, storage, tour planning, representation and international distribution. Authors receive 50% of all gross monies received.

Authors working with Pride literary agents will receive complete industry representation for 12% of gross royalties received.

Artists working with Pride novels receive advance payment for their art in addition to royalties on all two dozen products that will feature their art. Artists working with Pride children's books receive royalties equal to the author's.

Author submissions: Send complete manuscript, typed, single-sided, double-spaced on white paper. Resume and bio. Summary of entire manuscript. SASE for return of manuscript.

Artist submissions: Send five to ten color and black-and-white samples of artwork. Resume and bio. Cover letter discussing what types of projects you are interested in working on. SASE for response.

Matters of Pride

Novels, Poetry and Plays

Books brought to you by Pride Publications, our cutting-edge division.

Sweet Dark Places. Poetry. Lesléa Newman. Exploring the places of anger, and rage, fear and longing and most of all, the place of love in so many women readers. Less than two hundred copies left in print!
ISBN 0-939821-01-X $8.95

Love Me Like You Mean It. Poetry. Lesléa Newman. A collection rich with culture, memories, humor and spice, both sexy and powerful. These poems are touchstones to the vital transitions in a woman's life. Less than two hundred copies left in print!
ISBN 1-878533-14-2 $8.95

At the Edge. Play. Jennifer DiMarco. You'll laugh out loud. You'll shout hallelujah. Therese Weaver is a poet giving new meaning to the word "melodrama," and Daniel O'Donald is an HIV+ construction worker and activist. When these two women meet tectonic plates shift.
ISBN 1-886383-11-1 $9.95

The Redemption of Corporal Nolan Giles. Historical Fiction. Jeane Heimberger Candido. A rich, haunting tale set during the Civil War by a talented writer and Civil War enthusiast. The Civil War has never come alive as it does on these pages. Prepare yourself for the truth.
ISBN 1-886383-14-6 $11.95

talking drums. Prose Poetry. Jan Bevilacqua. Poems of love, life, sex and empowerment. Exploring gender and butch/femme in our society today. Features fourteen artplates by Kateren Lopez.
ISBN 1-886383-13-8 $9.95

1000 Reasons You Might Think She Is My Lover. Erotica. Angela Costa. Romantic, rowdy, tasty and titillating. A red-hot, pocket-sized collection that will make you laugh, blush... and look for a lover.
ISBN 1-886383-21-9 $10.95

Period Pieces. Poetry. Rudy Kikel. The third collection from this award-winning poet. Kikel uses characters from *Hamlet* to examine relationships, chronicles one family's dream of emigration and uses a framework of personal ads to explore how we say 'yes' and 'no.'
ISBN 1-886383-25-1 $9.95

Annabel and I. Romantic Fantasy. Chris Anne Wolfe. Set on Chautauqua Lake, the tale of a love that transcends all time and all categories. Jenny-wren is from the 1980s but Annabel is from the 1890s. Features thirteen interior artplates by Chris Storm.

ISBN 1-886383-17-0 $10.95

Bitter Thorns. Adult Fairytale. Chris Anne Wolfe. Magical, sensual retelling of Beauty and the Beast with two heroines. *From the Lion Fairytale Series*, #1. Features eight interior artplates by Lupa.

ISBN 1-886383-12-X $10.95

***Queen's Champion.* Adult Fairytale. Cris Newport. A classic and enticing retelling of Lancelot and Guinevere's love affair and the legend of Lancelot with a twist! *From the Lion Fairytale Series*, #2.

ISBN 1-886383-20-0 $11.95

The White Bones of Truth. Future Fiction. Cris Newport. In a future where film stars are owned by the Studio and independence is illegal, revolution brews. A novel of rock 'n' roll, redemption and virtual reality. Features five interior artplates by Pride Publications.

ISBN 1-886383-15-4 $10.95

Fall Through the Sky. Future Fiction. Jennifer DiMarco. In this stand-alone sequel to the bestselling adventure *Escape to the Wind*, Tyger and her gang the Windriders discover incredible secrets and prepare to face the Patriarchy.

ISBN 1-886383-16-2 $12.95

Children's Books
Books brought to you by Little Blue Works, Pride's children's division.

The Magical Child. Carol DiMarco and Connie Wurm. In the days of castles and kings, dragons and things, there lived a little girl named Angela Marie who was magic but didn't know it... yet! (Twenty-six pages. Ready-to-be-colored.)

ISBN 1-886383-19-7 $10.95

The Best Thing. Jennifer Anna and Joey Marsocci. With help from a magical key to Ladybug Land, two sisters discover the best thing in the world — each other! (Sixty pages. Ready-to-be-colored.)

ISBN 1-886383-26-X $12.95

Send check or money order to:
Pride Publications
Post Office Box 148
Radnor, Ohio 43066-0148